Girlness

Deal with it

body and soul

Diane Peters • Illustrated by Steven Murray

James Lorimer & Company Ltd., Publishers
Toronto

The neighbourhood guys are playing

baseball in the park. You grab your mitt and lace up your sneakers. "Can I play?" you ask. "I'm best in left field."

One boy shakes his head. "No girls. We need players who can hit hard and run fast." You tell everyone that you play for your school team and you're really good, but no one listens. It's not fair.

You have just been excluded because you're a girl.

People often make up their minds about what you are able to do because of your gender — whether you're a guy or a girl. When people treat you differently because of your gender, it's discrimination. If anyone ever tells you how you should be feeling, what role you should play, or how you should dress because of your gender, that's discrimination, too.

Gender discrimination happens to girls a lot.

People can have different ideas about what it means to be feminine. These differences can cause conflict and hurt feelings. They can make you change the way you act and feel — sometimes without even noticing — just to make things go smoother. It is up to every person to decide for herself what it means to be a girl. This book can help you look differently at the gender rules around you.

If you've ever judged someone based on your own idea of what girlness is, or if someone has made a judgment about you because of your gender, this book can help.

Contents

What is

Everyone knows there are big differences between girls and guys.

Girlness is another way of saying femininity. And we all know what it takes to be feminine, right? It's about liking girly things and leaving the boy things to boys. Aren't real girls:

- into cooking, crafts, and other "homey" stuff?
- better at reading than science?
- likely to cry at the drop of a hat?
- agile rather than strong?
- into fashion, makeup and magazines?
- good with children and babies?
- better followers than leaders?
- not very mechanically minded?

Girlness?

But wait. There are lots of girls who don't fit every description on that list. There are lots of girls who:

- are crazy about cars, computers, and outdoor things
- hate babysitting
- are very physically strong
- like to build things
- get their best grades in math and science
- don't care about clothes or makeup
- were not born girls, but identify with some aspects of femininity
- captain their sports teams and other groups
- have trouble showing their emotions.

Being a girl is about a whole lot more than fitting into old-fashioned ideas about what a girl can or cannot do.

Girlness 101

APPEARANCE

SATYA GETS A COOL NEW HAIRCUT

That haircut makes Satya look like a little girl — or a boy.

Is she even into guys?

Ideas of *girlness* can be

LIKES/DISLIKES

Hi, Aunt Marla! Wow, the new baby's a real cutie!

Sure is!

I told Aunt Marla you'd take the baby for awhile.

She says you were fawning all over him, so I knew you wouldn't mind.

ABILITIES

IT'S "FROG DISSECTION" DAY IN SCIENCE CLASS

SCIENCE LAB-A

Eew!

Gross!

Alicia's lab partner is away. Can I get someone to help her out?

I'm okay. I've already read the chapter and I know what I'm doing.

I'll do it.

BEHAVIOUR

ANNA'S GRAND-MOTHER IS VERY SICK...

AND ANNA CAN'T SEEM TO THINK ABOUT ANYTHING ELSE.

Geometry 3.9

D

Anna, this isn't up to your usual work. Do you want to talk about it?

based on . . .

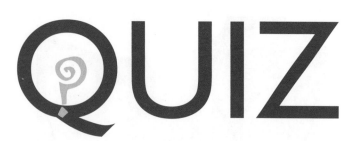

QUIZ

Why is it important to think about girlness?

When we don't define femininity for ourselves, we can get stuck with gender stereotypes. Stereotypes are pre-set ideas about groups of people and they can lead to discrimination. Another term for gender discrimination is sexism, which mostly describes treating girls or women differently than guys, or excluding them because they're female. In the following situations, is someone being discriminated against because of their gender? Check out the answers on the opposite page.

1 Lisa loves shoes, and spends every cent she makes on them. "You're such a girl!" her best friend laughs whenever she shows up in a new pair.

2 Pretty, blonde Nicola shows up for the first meeting of the debating club. The instructor has to decide right away who can go to the first meet, which is just two weeks away. Nicola gets passed over.

3 When Ming challenges a guy friend to a match at the local arcade, he laughs, "Girls can't play video games!" He doesn't laugh anymore when Ming wins the challenge.

4 Laura gets a new job as stockperson at the local drugstore, but then her boss assumes the boxes are too heavy for her to lift. She ends up working behind the cash register and hates it.

5 Kiki offers to help at the big school concert. She is given the job of seating people. One of the parent volunteers asks that all the girls wear makeup.

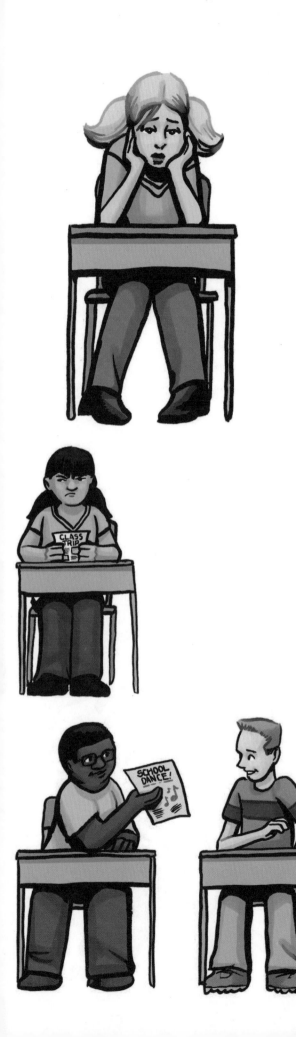

6 Aadi is very upset. She just found out that her grandfather started education funds for her brother and her two male cousins, but no money has been set aside for her and her female cousin.

7 Joline is excited about the big school trip, and about staying in a hotel. But then she finds out that the boys and girls will be staying in separate parts of the hotel, with the boys closer to the pool and in rooms with a better view.

8 Kalini knows her parents want her to marry someone from her own culture. Her parents won't even let her go to a dance with boys from other cultural backgrounds.

9 Tashi's health class gets divided up: the girls go with the female nurse to hear about sex and puberty, while the boys stay with the male teacher.

10 Naomi is the youngest child in her family, and the only girl. The whole family is crazy about motorcycles, and all Naomi's brothers ride, but their parents won't ever let Naomi try for her motorcycle license.

Answers

1. No. Lisa's friend is just joking around with her. It's only a problem if Lisa starts defining her value in the world by how good she — and her feet — look.

2. Yes, if the instructor assumed Nicola wasn't smart because she was pretty and blonde.

3. No. Ming's friend expressed a gender stereotype, but no one prevented Ming from playing the game or showing her real skills.

4. Yes. Laura's boss made an assumption about her abilities because she is a girl, limiting Laura's opportunity to do what she wants.

5. No. This parent is reinforcing a gender stereotype — that girls ought to wear makeup — and asking Kiki to do things she might not be comfortable with. But unless this parent makes Kiki leave her job or forces her to wear makeup this is not discrimination.

6. Yes. It's a very old idea that boys should get a good education and that girls either don't need one or aren't smart enough to handle one.

7. No. It's probably for safety and discipline reasons that the girls and boys are being kept apart, and the boys are just lucky that their rooms seem nicer.

8. No. It's not sexism if the boys in Kalini's family must follow the same rules. Kalini's parents might be discriminating against the boys Kalini knows, but that is cultural discrimination, not sexism.

9. No. Sometimes it's less embarrassing for girls and guys to be separated, especially when topics like sex are discussed.

10. Yes. It is sexism if Naomi is the same age that her brothers were when they got their licenses. If the only difference between Naomi and her brothers is gender, then not letting Naomi show that she can ride as well and as safely as her brothers is sexist.

Dear Girlness Counsellor

Q: I am the best hockey player at my school. There's no good league for me to play in, except the boys' league. I know I can handle it, and can outplay a lot of those boys. But no one will even let me try out! — *Left of Centre*

A: Other female athletes have faced this problem. Sometimes the problem is that places like hockey rinks don't have change rooms for girls. But mainly the argument is that boys tend to grow bigger and stronger than girls, and so girls have a harder time competing with boys and risk getting hurt. Remember, you should be judged on your own abilities, not whether you are a boy or a girl. Keep pushing for a tryout, but look for other fair solutions, too. Try to start a coed team, or an elite girls' team, to play on.

Q: My friend goes to an all-girl school. Is it sexist when schools or clubs teach only girls or guys?
— *The Coed*

A: It depends on the reason. Lots of schools accept only one gender because they feel that having the opposite gender around will distract students from their studies. And some clubs, like Boy Scouts and Brownies are just for boys or just for girls. Girls and guys sometimes have more fun and feel less stressed when they're apart. But if you're ever shut out of a group because of your gender and there's no good reason — and there's no similar group just for girls — the group is probably discriminating against you.

Q: Since I was a little girl, I've dreamed of becoming a police officer. My mother is very traditional: she thinks this job is unladylike and she thinks that no one will want to marry me if I have a man's job. What should I do?
— *Armed and Worried*

A: First you should talk to your mother and find out all of her reasons for objecting to a career in law enforcement for you. It might be that she is worried about your safety, and would feel the same way if you were her son instead of her daughter. Or she may have grown up at a time and in a place where powerful women who wore pants and carried weapons were not considered ideal wives. Try to open her eyes to how much things have changed. You might have to work hard, but speak calmly with her about how a police career would suit you and make you feel that you are making a difference. Tell her you are confident that, if you want to get married, there will be plenty of men who will find your strength and success very attractive.

Q: Last month, I went to my elementary school graduation. I really didn't want to wear a dress, but my mom made me. She said all the other girls would be wearing them, and she was right. Is this a rule I didn't know about? And is it sexist?
— *Gussied Up*

A: While I'm sure there are no rules saying you have to wear a dress to your graduation, it's a custom for everyone to dress up for a formal event. It's not sexism unless there are not similar expectations for the boys — I bet some of the guys wore jackets and ties. Next time, if you would be more comfortable wearing something else, suggest you and your mother shop for an alternative, like dress pants.

Myths

Only males can discriminate against females.

Anyone with pre-set ideas about what a girl can or cannot do could discriminate against her.

Girls are hardwired to be "feminine."

Some people believe that parents and teachers raise girls to have certain traits, or "nurture" ideas about girlness. Whether these traits are based on "nurture," "nature," or some combination of both, it is unfair to limit a girl to them, or to say a lack of them makes a girl unfeminine.

There are laws about discriminating against women, so it doesn't exist anymore.

Laws at schools and workplaces have helped break down limits put on women, but laws don't change what's in people's minds. Acts of discrimination against women still happen.

DID YOU KNOW?

- On average, women still make less money than men — about 79 cents for every dollar a man makes.

GIRLS are weaker than boys.

Most — but not all — grown women are physically smaller and not as strong as grown men. But a woman can become physically powerful, too. And there are other forms of strength that are not related to gender at all.

Because women have babies, they will always have limited choices.

Women can choose to have babies. They can also choose what they want to do with their lives, before or after they become mothers.

You're only a girl if you were born a girl.

Some people are a gender that does not match the gender they were assigned at birth. A person is a girl if that's what she knows she is, no matter what her birth certificate says.

- Gender discrimination can contribute to low self-esteem, depression, and eating disorders in girls.

- In the US, many women lost the right to vote by the early 1800s. In 1920 the vote was regained by women.

Hey, you love being a girl!

It doesn't bother you that boys are different from girls — that's natural. Sure, sometimes it's a drag spending so much time and money on how you look. And sometimes you envy how easy guys seem to have it — the way they just throw on their clothes in the morning, don't worry about what they eat, seem to be able to say whatever comes to mind. But if you want to one of the popular girls, that's what it takes, right? You're not a victim of gender discrimination

. . . right?

✓ Do question all stereotypes about gender.

✓ Do look past how people look and dress.

✓ Do educate yourself about the history of feminism.

✓ Do think about the similarities between boys and girls.

✓ Do think for yourself.

✓ Do remember that discrimination hurts everyone.

✓ Do choose your words carefully to make sure you're not using hurtful language.

✓ Do consider how gender discrimination has affected you and the girls around you.

✗ Don't make assumptions based on gender.

✗ Don't judge people by how they look.

✗ Don't automatically believe gossip about other girls.

✗ Don't be closed-minded about differences between people.

✗ Don't assume older traditions are better.

✗ Don't see people as just part of a group instead of as individuals.

QUIZ

Are you your own girl?

Are you the perfect girl on your own terms? It can be hard to know if you're just being you or if you're changing your behaviour because of the messages about femininity that are all around you. Take this quiz and see what you can find out. Of the following statements, how many are true, how many are false?

1. I like to look a way that helps me fit in.

2. I get intimidated when I have to build things or use technology or tools.

3. Girls who yell or talk loudly make me very uncomfortable.

4. We don't need more women in government or leading big companies.

5. Girls have different rights than boys.

6. I respect men in authority more than women.

7. I find it creepy when a girl dresses like and acts like a boy.

8. There's nothing wrong with a girl wearing skimpy clothes to get a guy's attention.

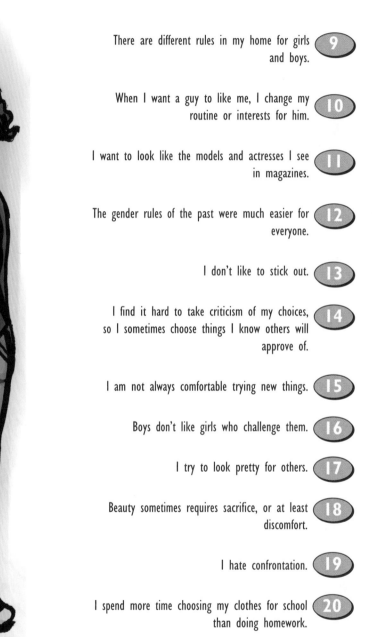

There are different rules in my home for girls and boys. **9**

When I want a guy to like me, I change my routine or interests for him. **10**

I want to look like the models and actresses I see in magazines. **11**

The gender rules of the past were much easier for everyone. **12**

I don't like to stick out. **13**

I find it hard to take criticism of my choices, so I sometimes choose things I know others will approve of. **14**

I am not always comfortable trying new things. **15**

Boys don't like girls who challenge them. **16**

I try to look pretty for others. **17**

Beauty sometimes requires sacrifice, or at least discomfort. **18**

I hate confrontation. **19**

I spend more time choosing my clothes for school than doing homework. **20**

Did you score a lot of Trues? Maybe it's time to start thinking about how you treat people who don't follow the gender rules as you see them, and to talk to someone about how your definition of girlness might be limiting you.

How to Harness Your Girl Power

There are lots of things you can do to make it easier for girls (and guys) to be whatever they choose.

Refuse to join or support clubs or group activities that exclude girls for no good reason. Or start up a girls' version of the same club or group.

Watch your language. When we're angry, or even when we're cracking jokes, words can come out of our mouths that show negative stereotypes about girlness — words like "slut" and phrases like "stop being such a girl." Remember: just because you don't mind these words doesn't mean

someone else won't be offended. You don't have to tolerate these jokes from others, either.

You know that saying, "what's good for the goose is good for the gander"? If you're not sure if

something is unfair, reverse the genders and think about the situation that way.

Stay aware. Take the time to think about things happening around you. If you stop, take a breath, and examine

events, you might better understand whether discrimination is happening.

Look past the surface. Think about the girls around you as being about more than just their clothes.

DID YOU KNOW?

• About **80%** of TV ad voice-overs are by men. Men voice **63%** of political ads, mostly about policies instead of personal attack ads.

When the Media is Involved

It isn't just family, friends, and teachers who send us messages about girlness. The media plays a part. Think of how much time you spend watching movies or TV, playing video games, listening to music, and reading magazines. What if these things are sending you messages about femininity that are outdated, unfair, or just plain wrong?

The people who create the media are often trying to sell products, attract advertisers, or make something as exciting and sexy as possible so people will like it. As a result, the media often portrays girls in stereotypical ways. Here are some things the media tells us about girlness:

- Girls must be very thin to be attractive.
- Heavier girls have no self-control.
- Being attractive is the most important thing about a girl.
- Being fashionable means having brand new clothes all the time.
- A girl's goal in life is to attract a hot guy.
- For a girl to attract a successful guy, she's got to look great and be in perfect control of her life.
- Smart girls are not attractive and don't have fun.

So what can you do about this? Break down how much time and money you spend on the media, and compare this with what you think is really important in your life. Try to:

- Cut back your intake of influences such as TV, video games, fashion magazines, and web sites.
- Increase your time reading books, especially those that contain positive images of girls.
- Start discussing the things you see and read with family and friends.
- Boycott media that portray women in really offensive ways; for example, certain music videos or video games.
- Question everything you see and read.
- Remember that female celebrities often go to extreme measures to look good.
- On social media, pay attention to who has uploaded a message or picture — and why. Are they selling something, pushing a celebrity, just trying to get you to click?
- Remind yourself constantly that you are worth more than your appearance.

Question assumptions like these: the girl who's into fashion is dumb; the tomboy is not feminine.

Share your feelings. Talk to friends or family about gender issues. Get many different points of view as you start thinking differently about this problem.

- In the early 1970s, **40%** of university students were women. Today, they represent **57%**.

- On the average day, **49%** of women do some kind of housework, compared to **20%** of men.

- Most of us learn about gender roles from our parents.

Sometimes it's hard being a girl.

You get so many mixed messages from all around you: be sensitive and strong, be caring and competitive, be attractive and assertive (but not too assertive). Often, you feel like you fall short of people's expectations of you. It seems like there are a million ways to be a girl — and you just don't fit.

Confusion about girlness can have a big impact on your life. It can

- make you want to change the way you dress
- limit the things you can do
- cause you to question your own abilities
- make you feel small
- make you wish you were a guy
- cause you to tone down your opinions and ideas
- make you wonder if you're still a girl
- lead you to worry that no one will find you attractive or lovable
- make you think your appearance is the most important thing.

DEAR DR. SHRINK-WRAPPED...

Q. I'm always getting picked on, and getting called things like "dyke" and "butch." I don't dress like other girls and I'm into different things, like sports and video games, but I don't think I'm interested in girls that way. Why can't people just leave me alone and let me be who I am?
— *Not Quite a Girl*

A. Dr. Shrink-Wrapped thinks this is a sad situation. It's very difficult to be under a lot of pressure to be just like everyone else. People who tease others about being different usually

- feel insecure about their own identity
- try to make someone else look or feel bad so they can feel better
- envy the person they're making fun of
- make fun of someone's approach to gender because their own gender identity has not been figured out yet.

It's this last one that makes some people call you those names. Lots of young people worry what others might be thinking about their own sexuality, so they spread the stereotype that if a girl dresses or looks a certain way, she must be a lesbian. Lesbians have romantic relationships with other women, but that doesn't make them any less feminine than women who have sexual feelings for men.

Your best bet is to ignore any petty comments. Do confront or report anything that is really hurtful or might lead you to be a victim of homophobia (when gays and lesbians are treated differently because of their sexuality). And surround yourself with friends who respect and care about who you are and how you choose to live.

Q. Now that I'm thinking about gender discrimination, I see it everywhere I go. I feel like there are a lot of things I can't do because I'm a girl. Why is the world so unfair?
— *Trapped as a Girl*

A. Dr. Shrink-Wrapped has news for you: life can be difficult, but that difficulty is not always because of gender discrimination. If a person says mean or stereotypical things about girls, or has in the past, that's one good clue that what you're facing is gender discrimination. But there are many reasons for getting excluded, not getting along with someone, not getting what we want, or getting picked on or teased.

What's most important, Trapped, is that you should not be the one doing the trapping. Even if other people think you can't do certain things because you're a girl, don't change your dreams or stop doing the things you love.

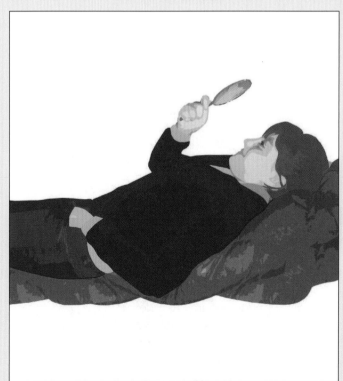

The **Out-Girl**

QUIZ

How do you cope with sexism?

Do you get angry? Clam up? Or start talking? Standing up for yourself and telling people how you feel is an empowered way to react to discrimination. You can also write a letter, form a club, or negotiate change. Here are some situations in which girlness is defined in different ways. Choose how you would react, then check at the end to see if you've opted for an empowered approach.

① FASHION TALK

You like to be comfortable, so you always wear what some people call guys' clothes. Now, people at school have started teasing you and have even posted stuff on the Internet about your sexuality. What do you do?
a) Start wearing more feminine clothes?
b) Report the gossip to adults?
c) Post rumours about the people teasing you?

② Hopped out

It was a fun party until someone started streaming YouTube videos on the TV. You are offended by the women in the music videos dancing around nearly naked and fawning over the men. Should you: a) Talk in private to the host of the party and ask for the videos to be turned off?
b) Start making fun of the videos and calling them stupid? c) Sit and watch, embarrassed, and eventually leave?

③ You Sexy Thing

Your favourite aunt gave you a new shirt for your birthday. Although it's tighter than you're used to, you wear it to class. All the boys are whispering nasty comments behind your back, and one guy grabs at your breasts! What should you do? a) Slap him? b) Report the improper touching to the teacher or principal? c) Slink away and never wear a tight shirt again.

④ Not adding up

Some younger students at school need math tutoring. You've got the best math marks in the class, but the teacher picks out two boys to be considered for the job. Should you: a) Freak out in class about the unfairness of it all? b) Complain to your friends after school? c) Immediately talk to the teacher and find out why he skipped over you (and report him if he doesn't have a good reason or change his mind)?

⑤ SLEEPING BAGGED

Your dad and uncle have planned an amazing camping trip for you and your cousins. When it turns out that you're the only girl who can make it, your parents decide you should stay home. How do you react?
a) Sulk and stomp around the house for a week? b) Say nothing?
c) Call a family meeting and talk about your parents' decision?

6 SICK BED

Your parents and two brothers go to visit your grandfather on a day that you're busy. You find out that he's very sick, and that they picked the time to visit so that you wouldn't come along. "We thought you'd be too emotional," your parents say. Should you: a) Yell at them all? b) Explain how you're feeling and insist on being taken to visit your grandfather? c) Go to your room and cry?

7 Kicking It

Every day at lunch, the boys take over the soccer field. You have organized a daily game with a group of girls, but you have no place to play. Should you: a) Talk to the boys about sharing the field? b) Report the boys to the principal? c) Cancel your game?

8 setting the stage

The church play needs lots of volunteers, so you have brought your toolbox to help build sets. But they keep sending you over to work on the costumes. Should you: a) Discuss your interests and skills with the adult in charge? b) Make costumes, but tell your friends how upset you are? c) Storm out?

9 The Bitch

You have strong opinions and are not afraid to state them. Your close friends tell you that people are calling you a loudmouth and a bitch behind your back. What should you do? a) Get even louder and repeat the insults in front of everyone? b) Try to tone down your personality? c) Ask your friends to speak out against the mean comments when they hear them?

10 CAREER PAIN

You have decided you want to be a doctor, but when you tell the guidance counsellor about your plans, he says your math and science marks are not high enough. You know you can get your marks up if you try, but the counsellor says that teenage girls have too much of a social life to be able to buckle down and study. He sends you off with pamphlets about a career in nursing. How do you react? a) Post nasty things about him on the Internet? b) Complain to the school and make another appointment with a different counsellor? c) Consider nursing?

Answers

An empowered reaction to these situations would be:

I. b	4. c	7. a	10. b
2. a	5. c	8. a	
3. b	6. b	9. c	

23

There are some simple things you can do
to protect yourself against gender discrimination.

Know your rights

If you think you're being discriminated against at school or at a job, you might be able to take legal steps. Do some research to find out what is considered right or wrong in your particular situation and what you can do about it.

Speak up

Whenever you can, tell the person who's discriminating against you how you feel. Make sure you feel safe and protected when you stand up for yourself. Use calm language and avoid calling people names — that way, you're more likely to be heard.

Get support

Talk to your friends and family about what's been happening. Make sure they support you in who you are and how you define girlness for yourself. Never change yourself just to make life easier.

DID YOU KNOW?

- In TV ads aimed at girls, **70%** are set at home. But boys in ads are shown at home only **27%** of the time.

do's and don'ts

✓ Do be proud of who you are and how you define femininity for yourself.

✓ Do share your concerns with your parents or an adult you can trust.

✓ Do learn about gender discrimination and the history of feminism.

✓ Do experiment with how you see girlness.

✓ Do accept others who are different than you.

✓ Do practise standing up for yourself in all situations.

✓ Do question all stereotypes about girls.

✓ Do look for good role models and follow their examples.

✗ Don't change the way you dress or what you like to do just to please others.

✗ Don't let stereotypes affect the way you value yourself.

✗ Don't discriminate back against other girls or boys.

✗ Don't let gender rules limit or change your hopes and dreams.

✗ Don't bottle up your feelings and become angry.

✗ Don't think of your gender as a trap.

✗ Don't blame gender discrimination for all your problems.

✗ Don't "judge a book by its cover."

Respect yourself
Never let gender stereotypes or discrimination affect how you feel about yourself. If someone has outdated ideas, that says more about them than it does about you. Remember you have value for many reasons, not just because of your looks or what you do for others.

- The average American woman lives 81 years, and the average man 76 years.

- Young girls and teens who read fashion magazines are twice as likely to diet and three times as likely to exercise to lose weight than those who don't.

The **Witness**

Ever witness a girl being teased, bullied, or excluded because of ideas about girlness?

Did you say anything? Do anything about it?

Well, why not?

The Power of Silence

It's scary to speak up when you don't like what you see around you. You worry about the consequences of accusing people of discrimination and standing up for a victim of sexism. You might get teased, lose friends, get told off, or cause someone to get in trouble. But when you say nothing, it's almost like you're saying, "It's okay. What you're doing is fine by me."

Start the Change

Speaking up when you've been a witness to discrimination is hard work. You may feel like what you have to say is not important and won't do anything. But change can start with one person.

✓ Do learn how to identify gender discrimination.

✓ Do feel you have a voice and an ability to affect the world around you.

✓ Do speak your mind if you feel safe enough to do so.

✓ Do tell a trustworthy adult about discrimination you've witnessed.

✓ Do educate yourself about women's rights.

✓ Do offer support and friendship to the target of discrimination.

✓ Do support those around you who are different.

✓ Do talk to your friends when you see them acting in sexist ways.

✓ Do keep an open mind about what girlness means.

✗ Don't change your behaviour to get along better with others.

✗ Don't stay silent.

✗ Don't hide your feelings when you've witnessed discrimination.

✗ Don't use sexist language.

✗ Don't encourage discrimination by laughing at sexist jokes or spreading gossip.

27

The **Witness**

QUIZ

Do you really get it?

You have an open mind about girlness and a strong sense of fairness. So, what do you do when you witness someone else dealing with discrimination? Take this quiz to see how you'd react in some high-pressure situations. This quiz has no right or wrong answers, because each situation is unique. Your answers may be different from the ones given below, but they could be right under the circumstances.

There's a new, secret group at school just for guys. There are no reasons why girls aren't being allowed, and it's becoming a place where guys go to talk about how they're superior and deserve more privileges at school.

- Talk to some group members. Let them know you think this is wrong.
- Let a trustworthy teacher know about this secret group. You might not have to name names, but let the teacher know it's going on.
- Ask the school to have open discussions about gender.

2 LABOUR WOES

Your boss is really sexist. You notice that he hires only girls who are pretty and curvy, and they must wear tight uniforms. He treats the guys with a lot more respect. The boys often get promoted, but never the girls.

- Talk to your parents. See if you have grounds to write a formal complaint.
- Talk to your co-workers about this problem. You might be able to work out a solution.
- Refuse to wear the tight uniform, and get as many of the other girls as you can to do the same. (Wear neat, clean clothes that your boss cannot object to.)

3 #STUPIDSHALLOW

One of the prettiest and most fashionable girls in school has become a target on an Instagram chat called #stupidshallow, with people complaining about her.

- Insist the chat be shut down and report it to your school.
- Online bullying is illegal and the police could get involved.
- Spearhead more positive conversations on social media.
- Get to know this girl and look beyond what others have said.
- Encourage her to be herself and not change her looks or personality to please others.

4 By the Book

In class, you're studying a book that seems pretty sexist to you. But week after week, the teacher says nothing. You're starting to feel uncomfortable, and suspect that the teacher silently believes what's in this book.

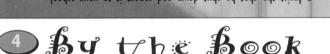

- Ask the teacher to have a class discussion about books and gender.
- Write an essay on the book's attitudes about women.
- Talk to your classmates about the book and how it makes you feel.
- Discuss this book with your parents. They might be able to help if you can't effect change yourself.

5 THE BATHROOM WALL

You're a guy, and you're really tired of what's written all over the guys' bathroom at school — really awful stuff about girls, and untrue stories about girls you know.

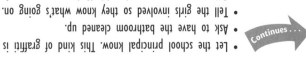

- Let the school principal know. This kind of graffiti is vandalism.
- Ask to have the bathroom cleaned up.
- Tell the girls involved so they know what's going on.
- Offer your support to the girls if they want to confront the guys involved.

Continues . . .

⑥ ROCK ON

Your little sister wants to be a musician. She's played your cousin's guitar a few times and seems to have a lot of talent! But your parents say it's not ladylike, and will only pay for piano or ballet lessons for her.

- Work with your sister to convince your parents that the guitar is an instrument for girls <u>and</u> guys.
- Do some research and inform your sister and your parents about some famous and accomplished women guitarists.
- Explain why you think the situation is unfair.

⑧ **Queen Diva**

There's a girl at school who's always targeting other girls who don't fit in. If they wear clothes that aren't just like hers, she makes fun of them.

- Let her targets know that she is just a bully, and not to take it personally.
- Stick up for the people she's making fun of.
- Let a trustworthy adult know that this bullying is hurting others.

⑦ *FB = Full of Baloney*

You friend a Facebook identity that turns out to be fake. The "person" posts things about girls at school, rating them on their clothes and even talking about their sexual activity.

- Report the fake account to authorities at school. They could report it to the police and have the account shut down.
- Tell the girls mentioned on the page about it.
- Refuse to spread any gossip you read there.
- Tell your friends you think the site is lame and full of lies.
- Ask the school to educate students about online bullying.

DID YOU KNOW❓

- It's been proven that countries who treat women as equals to men have faster- growing and healthier economies.

9 HOLIDAY HASSLE

It's a big family holiday dinner. Your oldest sister ends up slaving away in the kitchen while everyone else is having fun.

- Discuss with your parents how unfair you feel this is: the work should be divided evenly.
- Offer to do some of the work so your sister can enjoy herself. Give your mom a break, too, while you're at it.
- Make sure the next event is prepared for by everyone in the family equally.

10 RATED WRONG

You're a guy and your best friend has a weird way of talking about girls. He makes rude comments when girls walk by wearing tight clothes. He's even gone online to rate some of your female friends on whether or not they are hot.

- Avoid laughing at his comments or egging him on.
- Let him know that you are not comfortable talking about girls that way.
- Remind him that rating girls online could be considered cyberbullying, which is against the law.

- About **22%** of people in national parliaments around the world are women.

- While almost **70%** of students studying education and health in university are girls, females make up only **25%** of those studying math, engineering, and science.

- Over **80%** of girls diet before age 18; **40%** of 9-year-olds are dieting.

More **Help**

It takes time and practise to learn the skills in this book. There are many ways to deal with gender discrimination, but only you know what feels right for you in different situations. In the end, the best response is the one that prevents everyone from being hurt or treated unfairly.

If you need more information or someone to talk to, these resources might help.

Helplines

Kids Help Phone 1-800-668-6868

Justice for Children and Youth 1-866-999-JCFY

Girls and Boys Town National Hotline 1-800-448-3000

Web sites

The Canadian Safe School Network www.canadiansafeschools.com

Kids Help Phone www.kidshelpphone.ca

Boys Town www.boystown.org

Stop Bullying Now www.stopbullying.gov

Books

Big Night Out by Jeanne Beker. Tundra Books, 2005.

The Breadwinner by Deborah Ellis. Groundwood Books, 2000.

The Dear Canada Series by Jean Little, Maxine Trottier, and others. Scholastic Canada.

Delaying the Game by Lorna Schultz Nicholson. James Lorimer & Co., 2005.

Even if it Kills Me by Dorothy Joan Harris. Scholastic Canada, 2000.

The Evolution of Calpurnia Tate by Jacqueline Kelly. Square Fish, 2011.

Girl Fight by Faye Harnest. James Lorimer & Co., 2011.

The Hollow Tree by Janet Lunn. Seal Books, 2001.

In Your Face: The Culture Of Beauty And You by Shari Graydon. Annick Press, 2004.

Our Canadian Girl series by Anne Laurel Carter, Kathy Stinson, Lynne Kositsky, and others. Penguin Canada.

Pick and Roll by Kelsey Blair. James Lorimer & Co., 2014.

Soccer Star by Jacqueline Guest. James Lorimer & Co., 2003.

Stargirl by Jerry Spinelli. Scholastic, 2000.

Super Women in Science by Kelly Di Domenico. Second Story Press, 2002.

Two Strikes by Johnny Boateng. James Lorimer & Co., 2016.

White Lily by Ting-Xing Ye. Seal Books, 2003.

Find other titles in the Deal With It series at www.lorimer.ca/dealwithit

Additional © illustrations on pages:

1 – Ben Shannon

4 – crying: Remie Geoffroi; makeup: Dan Workman; shopping: Ben Shannon

5 – science: Dan Workman; plaid shirt: Nick Johnson

13 – birth certificate: Nick Johnson

14 – Jeremy Tankard

15 – girl thinking: Nick Johnson; whispering: Ben Shannon

19 – Ben Shannon

20 – Ben Shannon

21 – mirror: Dan Workman

22 – fashion: Ben Shannon

23 – soccer team & green shirt: Dan Workman

26 – Remie Geoffroi

27 – hands on hips: Ben Shannon; support: Dan Workman

30 – guitars: Remie Geoffroi

31 – keyboard: Geraldine Charette

Text copyright © 2005, 2017 by Diane Peters

Illustrations copyright © 2005, 2017 by Steven Murray

James Lorimer & Company Ltd., Publishers acknowledges the support of the Ontario Arts Council (OAC), an agency of the Government of Ontario. We acknowledge the support of the Canada Council for the Arts, which last year invested $153 million to bring the arts to Canadians throughout the country. This project has been made possible in part by the Government of Canada and with the support of the Ontario Media Development Corporation.

Design: Blair Kerrigan/Glyphics

Cover image: Shutterstock

Library and Archives Canada Cataloguing in Publication

Peters, Diane, author

    Girlness : deal with it body and soul / by Diane Peters ; illustrated by Steven Murray. -- [New edition]

(Deal with it)

Includes bibliographical references.

ISBN 978-1-4594-1186-9 (hardback)

    1. Girls--Psychology--Juvenile literature. 2. Femininity--Juvenile literature. 3. Gender identity--Juvenile literature. I. Murray, Steven, illustrator II. Title. III. Series: Deal with it (Toronto, Ont.)

HQ1229.P48 2017   j155.3'33   C2016-906888-9

James Lorimer & Company Ltd., Publishers

117 Peter Street, Suite 304

Toronto, ON, Canada

M5V 0M3

www.lorimer.ca

American edition published in 2017

Distributed by: Lerner Publishing Group

1251 Washington Ave N

Minneapolis, MN, USA

55401

Printed and bound in Hong Kong.